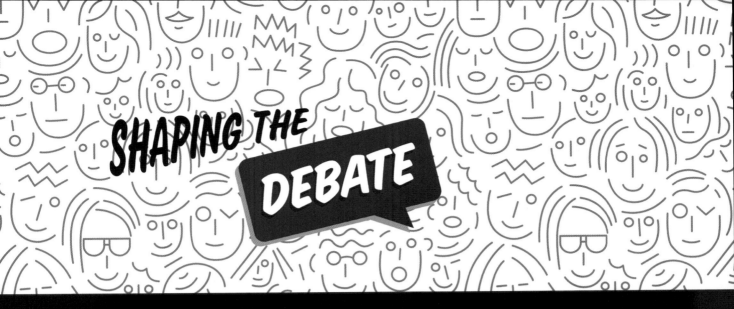

SHAPING THE DEBATE

Defining and Discussing
WOMEN'S RIGHTS

Christy Mihaly

Rourke
Educational Media

A Division of
Carson
Dellosa
Education®

rourkeeducationalmedia.com

ROURKE'S
SCHOOL to HOME
CONNECTIONS
BEFORE AND DURING READING ACTIVITIES

Before Reading: *Building Background Knowledge and Vocabulary*

Building background knowledge can help children process new information and build upon what they already know. Before reading a book, it is important to tap into what children already know about the topic. This will help them develop their vocabulary and increase their reading comprehension.

Questions and Activities to Build Background Knowledge:

1. Look at the front cover of the book and read the title. What do you think this book will be about?
2. What do you already know about this topic?
3. Take a book walk and skim the pages. Look at the table of contents, photographs, captions, and bold words. Did these text features give you any information or predictions about what you will read in this book?

Vocabulary: *Vocabulary Is Key to Reading Comprehension*

Use the following directions to prompt a conversation about each word.

- Read the vocabulary words.
- What comes to mind when you see each word?
- What do you think each word means?

Vocabulary Words:
- abolish
- advocate
- comprise
- constitute
- constitutional
- contraception
- exclude
- fundamental
- immigration
- intimidation
- mutilation
- opposed

During Reading: *Reading for Meaning and Understanding*

To achieve deep comprehension of a book, children are encouraged to use close reading strategies. During reading, it is important to have children stop and make connections. These connections result in deeper analysis and understanding of a book.

 Close Reading a Text

During reading, have children stop and talk about the following:

- Any confusing parts
- Any unknown words
- Text to text, text to self, text to world connections
- The main idea in each chapter or heading

Encourage children to use context clues to determine the meaning of any unknown words. These strategies will help children learn to analyze the text more thoroughly as they read.

When you are finished reading this book, turn to page 46 for Text-Dependent Questions and an Extension Activity.

TABLE OF CONTENTS

CHAPTER ONE

WOMEN: SECOND-CLASS CITIZENS?

On January 21, 2017, women around the world marched to demand equal rights. Speakers, celebrities, and hundreds of thousands of supporters gathered in the United States capital for the Women's March on Washington. As many as 5.2 million marchers demonstrated in cities nationwide. They shouted slogans such as "We're not going away" and "Girls rule!"

A crowd of Women's March demonstrators in Washington, D.C., stretches toward the Capitol Building.

These marches occurred the day after Donald Trump was inaugurated as U.S. President. During his campaign, Trump insulted women including comedian Rosie O'Donnell and businesswoman Carly Fiorina. He **opposed** federal health care laws, leading many Americans to believe that he would limit women's access to birth control and other medical care. Though his supporters said he treated women fairly, Trump made comments that many considered hostile to women.

Donald Trump was elected President of the United States in November 2016.

In the November 2016 election, Trump defeated Hillary Clinton. She was the first woman to run for U.S. President as the nominee of a major party. In her campaign, Clinton called for equal pay for men and women. She urged voters to help her break the glass ceiling that has prevented women from reaching the same high positions as men.

Hillary Clinton's presidential campaign was followed by a wave of activism by women in the United States.

Both candidates discussed **immigration**, national security, economic policies, and other issues. But for many Americans, the 2016 election shone a particular spotlight on inequalities in how men and women are treated. The women's marches signaled the start of a fresh conversation about women's rights.

What Do You Do?

Data from U.S. Government Survey of Jobs Held by Men and Women

Job	Percentage filled by women (in 2018)
Construction Laborers	3.7%
Firefighters	5.1%
Aircraft Pilots/Flight Engineers	9%
Computer Programmers	21.2%
Chief Executives	26.9%
Lawyers	37.4%
Physicians/Surgeons	40.3%
Advertising Sales Agents	50.4%
Flight Attendants	74.9%
Elementary/Middle School Teachers	79.8%
Paralegals/Legal Assistants	86.4%
Registered Nurses	88.6%.
Secretaries/Administrative Assistants	94%

CHAPTER TWO

A FEMALE HISTORY OF THE UNITED STATES

This woman, known as Pretty Nose, was probably Arapaho, although some have identified her as Cheyenne. It's said she participated in the 1876 Battle of the Little Bighorn, also called Custer's Last Stand, in which Lakota Sioux and Cheyenne warriors defeated United States forces.

Among American Indian cultures, women's roles varied. In some groups, women were leaders, active in tribal decision-making and governance. Certain tribes were matrilineal, meaning that family names and property passed down from the mother's side.

Among the Crow people, some women were respected warriors. This illustration depicts the Crow fighter known as Woman Chief.

European colonists brought their laws and customs to North America. In the seventeenth through nineteenth centuries, therefore, most American women couldn't own property, hold jobs, or vote. Only men could.

Women in the American colonies often worked long, hard hours alongside men, and were also expected to manage the home. They had very few legal rights, especially if married.

THE WOMEN OF '76.

"MOLLY PITCHER" THE HEROINE OF MONMOUTH.

Her husband falls—she sheds no ill timed tear, | The foe press on—she checks their mad career,
But firm resolved—she fills his fatal post. | Who can avenge like her a husband's ghost?.

The folk hero Molly Pitcher, shown here during battle, is representative of many women who supported the American forces in camps and on battlefields.

During the Revolutionary War, nonetheless, soldiers' wives sometimes followed their men into battle. Women also supported independence in other ways. Mercy Otis Warren, an early **advocate** of the revolution, held protest meetings in her home and wrote political plays and essays to persuade others to join the cause.

In the 1800s, women campaigned to **abolish** slavery. Most people at that time disapproved of females speaking in public. Maria Stewart, an African-American abolitionist, is believed to be the first American woman to give public political lectures. She was criticized for her talks in the 1830s, but she led the way for others. In the 1840s through 1890s, anti-slavery leaders such as Sojourner Truth and Susan B. Anthony were popular speakers.

Sojourner Truth escaped from slavery and became a prominent advocate for abolition and human rights.

Susan B. Anthony

Inspired by her belief in equality, Susan B. Anthony worked for the abolition of slavery and women's rights to vote. In 1872, she voted in the presidential election, and was arrested and fined for her illegal vote. Anthony spent more than 50 years seeking voting rights for women, but died in 1906, 14 years before the 19th Amendment gave women the vote.

Susan B. Anthony
1820–1906

Alice Paul was criticized as "unladylike" for her aggressive tactics in seeking the vote for women.

Beginning in the 1840s, women also fought for the right to vote. In the 1910s, Alice Paul and the National Woman's Party picketed the White House. They were jailed and beaten. Their sacrifices bore fruit when Congress passed the 19th Amendment to the Constitution to give women the right to vote. The amendment became effective in 1920 when 36 state legislatures ratified it.

Beginning in January 1917, women stood in front of the White House holding banners, putting political pressure on President Woodrow Wilson to support women's rights to vote. Many of these women were arrested and imprisoned for demonstrating.

YES, They Could

Many girls grew up hearing "Ladies can't do that!" Yet many followed their dreams anyway. These three women were the first in their previously male-only fields.

1849: Elizabeth Blackwell graduated from a U.S. medical school.

1916: Jeannette Rankin was elected to Congress.

1983: Sally Ride flew into space as an astronaut.

In the 1960s, women such as Rosa Parks and Fannie Lou Hamer played important roles in the civil rights movement. The 1960s also saw renewed interest in women's rights. In 1966, Gloria Steinem, Betty Friedan, and other feminists formed the National Organization for Women (NOW). NOW sought equality in employment, pay, and other areas, and campaigned for a **constitutional** amendment, the Equal Rights Amendment (ERA).

In 1955, Rosa Parks was arrested for refusing to give up her seat on a Montgomery, Alabama, bus to allow a white man to sit. She was arrested again in 1956 for helping organize a citywide bus boycott in Montgomery.

Betty Friedan's 1963 book, *The Feminine Mystique*, helped launch the women's movement.

Fannie Lou Hamer was a leader of the civil rights movement in Mississippi. In 1971 she co-founded the National Women's Political Caucus.

Starting in the 1950s, feminist Gloria Steinem worked for equality for women and girls. President Obama gave her the Presidential Medal of Freedom in 2013.

The ERA states: "Equality of rights under the law shall not be denied or abridged ... on account of sex." In 1972, the U.S. Congress passed this amendment. To become effective, an amendment must be ratified by three-fourths, or 38, of the states. Although 35 state legislatures approved the ERA within ten years, this fell short of the number required.

A conservative group, STOP ERA, organized the opposition to the ERA. It argued that women should follow the traditional roles of wife and mother, rather than pursuing careers.

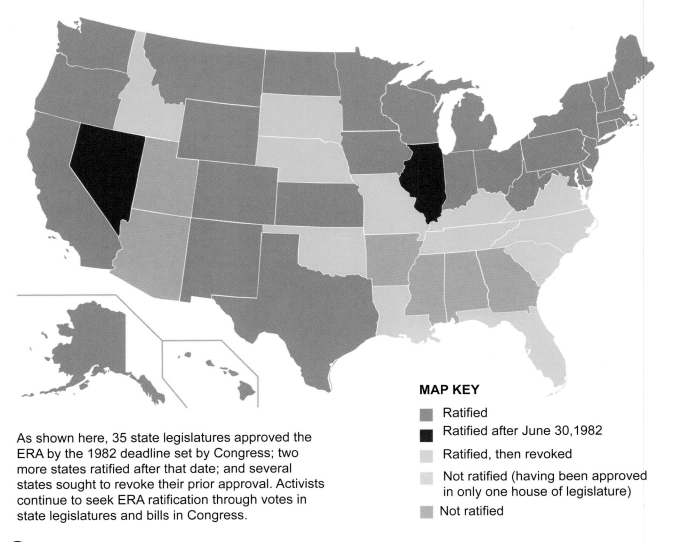

As shown here, 35 state legislatures approved the ERA by the 1982 deadline set by Congress; two more states ratified after that date; and several states sought to revoke their prior approval. Activists continue to seek ERA ratification through votes in state legislatures and bills in Congress.

MAP KEY

■ Ratified
■ Ratified after June 30, 1982
■ Ratified, then revoked
■ Not ratified (having been approved in only one house of legislature)
■ Not ratified

Phyllis Schlafly campaigned against the ERA, warning that under the amendment women would no longer have the right to support from their husbands.

Phyllis Schlafly

Phyllis Schlafly led STOP ERA. She complained that NOW represented the interests of young career women and betrayed older housewives and widows. She argued the ERA would require drafting women into the military, that it would damage family values, and that children would be taken from mothers after divorce.

CHAPTER THREE

THE GENDER GAP AROUND THE GLOBE

Worldwide, girls and women face patriarchies—legal and cultural systems that give greater power and privileges to men and boys. About 130 million girls ages 6 to 17 cannot attend school in many areas around the globe. In some countries, women can't own property. In Saudi Arabia, women need a male guardian's permission to work, travel, or attend school.

Countries with some of the highest rates of girls out of school include Eritrea, Liberia, Pakistan, and Syria.

In June 2018, women in Saudi Arabia were allowed, for the first time, to get driver's licenses. Saudi Arabia was the last country in the world to allow women to drive.

Malala Yousafzai

When Malala Yousafzai was growing up in Pakistan, the Taliban closed girls' schools. Malala publicly criticized the Taliban for depriving girls of education. In 2012, Taliban fighters boarded Malala's school bus and shot her. She recovered from serious injuries, won the 2014 Nobel Peace Prize, and continued defending girls' education.

In 2013, Malala Yousafzai and her father started Malala Fund, an organization that works to help more girls go to school.

19

In many countries, girls are forced into early marriage. The United Nations (UN) reports that in Niger, 28 percent of girls marry by age 15; 76 percent by age 18. Child brides often leave school, and their health is endangered if they get pregnant while very young. In fact, complications of pregnancy and childbirth are the leading cause of death among 15- to 19-year-old girls globally.

Among other effects, early marriage reduces the potential future earnings of child brides.

Another practice, which the World Health Organization (WHO) calls "an extreme form of discrimination against women and girls," is female genital **mutilation** (FGM). Practiced in about 30 countries in Africa, Asia, and the Middle East, FGM has traditionally been performed by women as a rite of passage. It involves cutting girls' external genital organs. This causes pain and injuries, and serves no medical purpose. WHO and other organizations are working to educate communities about the risks and encourage governments to ban the practice.

Established in 1948, the WHO is a special agency of the United Nations which works to promote the health of people around the world.

CHAPTER FOUR

WORKING TOWARD EQUALITY

The U.S. Constitution's 14th Amendment was adopted in 1868, after the Civil War, to protect the rights of formerly enslaved people. It promised equal protection to all. However, it was not immediately applied to women.

The 14ᵗʰ Amendment

No State shall make or enforce any law which shall abridge the privileges or immunities of citizens of the United States; nor shall any State deprive any person of life, liberty, or property, without due process of law; nor deny to any person within its jurisdiction the equal protection of the laws.

[excerpt of 14th Amendment, section 1]

Some Countries Ranking High and Low on the Equality Scale

Higher

Iceland: Parliament is almost half women; employers must certify they pay men and women equally.

Rwanda: Parliament is majority women; still, at home, females are pressured to conform to traditional roles.

Lower

Yemen: Ongoing war has worsened conditions for women and children, causing extreme shortages of food and medical supplies.

Pakistan: Females, especially in rural areas, are traditionally segregated and kept at home. Many lack education and access to health care.

In 1873, the Supreme Court ruled that a state could **exclude** women from practicing law. In 1924, it upheld a ban on women working as late-night waitresses. In 1961, a woman facing a jury trial wanted women sitting on her jury. The Supreme Court said she had no such right.

But the tide turned. In the 1960s, responding to the civil rights movement, Congress began extending equal protection to women. A 1963 statute required equal pay for equal work. The Civil Rights Act of 1964 banned employment discrimination based on sex.

The Supreme Court of the United States

In 1972, Congress prohibited sex discrimination in federally-funded schools—including in their sports programs. By 1975, the Supreme Court revisited the jury question, and ruled that states could not exclude women from juries.

Computers in Skirts

Before machine computers, women often performed mathematical calculations for scientists. In the 1870s through 1910s, the Harvard College Observatory generally wouldn't allow women to use its telescopes, but hired women to analyze and measure photographs of the stars. In the 1930s through 1960s, women couldn't be astronauts, but NASA hired women to compute astronauts' flightpaths.

In the late 19th and early 20th centuries, the low-paid female computers working for the Harvard College Observatory made many important contributions to astronomy. Modern astronomers still rely upon the observations and discoveries of Annie Jump Cannon, Henrietta Leavitt, and others from this group.

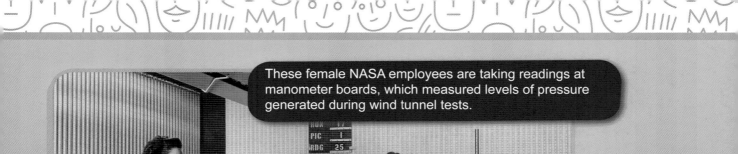

These female NASA employees are taking readings at manometer boards, which measured levels of pressure generated during wind tunnel tests.

Katherine Johnson worked as a NASA computer and aerospace technologist. She calculated the trajectories for Alan Shepard's 1961 flight and for Apollo 11's flight to the moon in 1969.

This photo from the 1950s shows a NASA employee working with an early calculator called a Friden machine.

In 1973, in *Roe v. Wade*, the Supreme Court decided a woman has a **fundamental** right to end her pregnancy. The court struck down a Texas law that banned most abortions. Texas argued that it was obliged to protect unborn fetuses. The court disagreed, stating that someone is a "person" for purposes of the 14th Amendment only after their birth.

Although recent opinion polls find most Americans agree that *Roe v. Wade* should stand, the case did not end the abortion debate. Pro-choice advocates believe that a woman's right to control her body, including deciding whether to continue a pregnancy, must be protected. Opponents argue that abortion is murder and that women must take responsibility for their pregnancies. Supporters of *Roe v. Wade* respond that without legal abortion, women would turn to unsafe, illegal ways to end pregnancies, risking death.

Activists demonstrate to protect women's access to clinics that offer abortions.

Demonstrators on the left of the photo express their support for ending abortions, while those on the right protest limitations on abortions.

CHAPTER FIVE

ONGOING ISSUES IN THE UNITED STATES

Many women rely on family planning (planning when to have children) to pursue education and careers. The 2010 Affordable Care Act (ACA) helped women by requiring health insurance to cover **contraception** and pregnancy care. The law barred denial of insurance on the basis of gender or pre-existing conditions. Under the ACA, millions of previously uninsured people received insurance covering family planning and other health care.

The ACA is often called "Obamacare" after President Barack Obama, who signed it into law. Health care reform was one of his top priorities.

Affordable Care Act

The Patient Protection and Affordable Care Act of 2010 (ACA) sought to lower federal spending on health care by encouraging people to seek preventive care.

Opponents argued the ACA was too expensive and raised taxes. They said the government should stay out of health care. In 2017, Republican efforts to repeal the ACA failed. A court decision in 2018 found the ACA unconstitutional. The debate over the law continued.

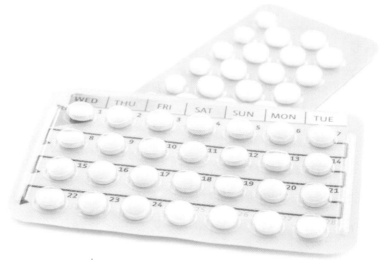

Birth control pills such as these are a common means of contraception.

People also disagree about public funding of Planned Parenthood, an organization providing health care to low-income women and men. Abortion opponents have sought to cut off its funding, because along with cancer screenings and pregnancy care, Planned Parenthood offers abortions. But others point out that U.S. law already prohibits use of federal funds for most abortions. Health care analysts warn that cuts to Planned Parenthood would reduce low-income patients' access to important health care services.

Supporters and opponents of Planned Parenthood make their opinions known with prayers and protests.

In 1984, President Ronald Reagan announced the U.S. would impose a "global gag rule," also called the Mexico City policy. In the years since then, Democratic presidents have rescinded this policy, while Republicans have reinstated it.

Global Gag Rule

Under the Trump administration, the U.S. applied a "global gag rule" to international health organizations that receive U.S. aid. It barred these organizations from providing abortions, or counseling about abortion. Studies showed this U.S. policy increased rates of unplanned pregnancies, abortions, and health complications, including women's deaths, in

Another ongoing discussion centers on sexual harassment and sexual assault. Sexual harassment includes verbal **intimidation**, threats or obscene remarks, and unwanted physical contact. Sexual assault is generally defined as touching someone in an intimate way, without consent.

Men and women across the country have participated in #MeToo demonstrations like this one in San Francisco.

The #MeToo movement ignited conversations about these issues in 2017. #MeToo encouraged people who had experienced sexual assault, even years earlier, to report it. Hundreds of thousands told their stories. Some people accused of assaults, mostly powerful men, were fired and/or faced criminal charges.

Many apologized for their conduct. Others issued denials. Some people complained it was too easy to make false accusations. Women and men alike began working to defend both victims of assaults and those falsely accused, and to foster healthy relationships and open communication about these issues.

Dr. Christine Blasey Ford

Brett Kavanaugh Hearings

During the 2018 U.S. Senate hearings on Supreme Court nominee Brett Kavanaugh, Dr. Christine Ford testified. She said Kavanaugh sexually assaulted her 30 years earlier. Kavanaugh denied this. The nation was divided over the issues raised: consent, assault, entitlement, fairness, courage, and honesty. The Senate voted 50-48 to confirm Kavanaugh.

After a stormy hearing and nationwide protests, Brett Kavanaugh was sworn in as a member of the Supreme Court. Retired Justice Anthony Kennedy administered the oath.

CHAPTER SIX

WHERE ARE WE HEADED?

In the 2018 midterm elections, U.S. women made history. Record numbers ran as candidates for state governors and members of Congress. For the first time, more than 100 women were elected to the House of Representatives. Yet women still **comprise** less than one quarter of Congress.

Faces from the Class of 2018

Rep. Deb Haaland (Democrat of New Mexico) belongs to the Pueblo of Laguna and was elected one of the first two American Indian women in Congress.

Rep. Sharice Davids (Democrat of Kansas), a member of the Ho-Chunk Nation, was the first person elected to Congress as both openly LGBT and American Indian.

Rep. Ilhan Omar (Democrat of Minnesota), an immigrant from Somalia, was elected one of the first two Muslim women in Congress.

Rep. Rashida Tlaib (Democrat of Michigan) became one of the first two Muslim women in Congress.

Gov. Kristi Noem (Republican of South Dakota) became her state's first female governor.

Sen. Marsha Blackburn (Republican of Tennessee) was the first woman elected to the U.S. Senate from her state.

Rep. Ayanna Pressley (Democrat of Massachusetts) was elected as the first African American Congresswoman from her state.

Rep. Alexandria Ocasio-Cortez (Democrat of New York) became the youngest woman ever elected to Congress.

Battle of the Sexes

In September 1973, women's tennis star Billie Jean King defeated former number-one-ranked player Bobby Riggs in a widely publicized match. Riggs had slammed the quality of women's tennis, boasting he could beat any woman. King's 6-4, 6-3, 6-3 victory over Riggs helped assure that women's tennis was taken seriously.

After their match, Riggs (right) said that Billie Jean King's tennis playing "was just too good for me."

Women continue working toward equality in athletics too. In 2018, the World Surf League, after years of pressure, announced it would award equal prize money to female and male winners. The U.S. Open tennis tournament pays men and women equally. But in most sports, women earn much less than men. Average pay for NBA (National Basketball Association) players is more than ten times that of WNBA (Women's National Basketball Association) players.

Air Force Colonel Merryl Tengesdal flies the U-2, one of the most challenging of all aircraft.

Though women still **constitute** a minority of the U.S. military, they are gradually integrating the armed forces. Until recently, women were banned from combat and could serve only in support roles. They can now train for combat positions, another step toward equality with men.

Advertisements like this from the late nineteenth century encouraged women to try bicycling.

Technology Helps Bring Equality

In the 1890s, the bicycle helped women gain confidence by giving them independent transportation. Now, in developing countries, bringing electricity and piped drinking water to communities liberates girls and women from household tasks like building cooking fires and fetching water. And the internet offers access to an education.

People support gender equality for various reasons. Many simply believe everyone deserves an equal chance. "Human rights are women's rights and women's rights are human rights," Hillary Clinton once famously said. And if women have more freedom, men do too. For example, where all careers are open to all, men may choose traditionally female occupations such as nursing or staying home with children. Further, countries where women have greater equality tend to have healthier economies. Equal rights for women can benefit everyone.

In 1995, First Lady Hillary Clinton delivered a strong message to China and the world, calling for an end to policies oppressing women. She spoke at the Fourth World Conference on Women, convened by the United Nations in Beijing, China.

Gender equality means that men as well as women have more options in their families and careers.

PRACTICE PREPARING FOR A DEBATE

People explain issues and solve problems through discussion. Debates are formal discussions about an issue. Debate participants present facts they have gathered from reliable sources. They present this information as they try to convince listeners that their opinions about an issue are correct.

Supplies

- paper
- pencil
- books on your topic and/or internet access

Directions:

1. Decide the topic you will research.

2. Write a question that will shape your debate. Example: Should religion be taught in public schools?

3. Write your proposition or opposition statement. Proposition example: Religion should be taught in public schools. Opposition example: Religion should not be taught in public schools.

4. Research your topic using a variety of sources. Make a list of the facts you find and note the source of each fact next to it.

5. Practice presenting your argument.

6. Flip the script! Follow steps 1–5 again, this time preparing with facts that support the other side.

Bonus: Form a debate club with your friends. Assign a new topic regularly. Give each person equal time to present their arguments.

Glossary

abolish (uh-BAH-lish): to end something officially

advocate (AD-vuh-kuht): a person who supports a plan, idea, or cause

comprise (kuhm-PRIZE): to make up or be part of

constitute (KAHN-sti-toot): to form or to make up

constitutional (kahn-sti-TOO-shuh-nuhl): having to do with a constitution, or the basic laws stating the rights of the people and powers of government

contraception (kahn-truh-SEP-shun): methods to prevent pregnancy

exclude (ik-SKLOOD): to keep someone from taking part in something

fundamental (fuhn-duh-MEN-tuhl): basic or important

immigration (im-i-GRAY-shuhn): moving from one country to settle in another

intimidation (in-ti-muh-DAY-shuhn): frightening people, especially to make them do something

mutilation (myoo-tuh-LAY-shuhn): an action injuring someone by damaging part of their body permanently

opposed (uh-POZED): stood against, tried to prevent, or disagreed with something

Index

Text-Dependent Questions

1. What were women's roles in the U.S. campaign to end slavery?
2. What are some countries where women have more, and less, equality with men?
3. What does the 14th Amendment to the U.S. Constitution provide?
4. What was *Roe v. Wade*?
5. What is the #MeToo movement?

Extension Activity

Imagine you work for the Department of Defense and have been asked to write a memo advising the Defense Secretary on whether women should be allowed to fight in combat. Formulate a recommendation to the Secretary, giving your reasons and considering the arguments on the other side too.

Bibliography

Chira, Susan, "The Women's March Became a Movement. What's Next?" *The New York Times*, Jan. 20, 2018.

Erickson, Amanda, Siobhán O'Grady, Ruby Mellen and Adam Taylor, "Women's Lives, Behind the Data." *The Washington Post*, Nov. 19, 2018.

Girls Not Brides website. https://www.girlsnotbrides.org/, (accessed December 28, 2018).

Mortimer, Caroline, "Number of Girls in Education Around the World Falls by Hundreds of Thousands." *Independent*, Oct. 10, 2017.

National Organization for Women (NOW) website, https://now.org/. (accessed December 27, 2018).

Oyez, "*Roe v. Wade*." https://www.oyez.org/cases/1971/70-18. (accessed December 28, 2018).

Quackenbush, Casey, "The Impact of President Trump's 'Global Gag Rule' on Women's Health is Becoming Clear." *Time*, Feb. 2, 2018.

Schwab, Klaus, "Global Gender Gap Report 2018." *World Economic Forum*. https://www.weforum.org/reports/the-global-gender-gap-report-2018. (accessed March 15, 2019).

U.S. Department of Labor, Bureau of Labor Statistics, "Labor Force Statistics from the Current Population Survey." https://www.bls.gov/cps/cpsaat11.htm. (last updated January 18, 2019).

Vagins, Deborah J, "Analysis: What the 2018 Midterm Results Mean for Women." *American Association of University Women*, Nov. 13, 2018. https://www.aauw.org/2018/11/13/analysis-what-the-2018-midterm-results-mean-for-women/.

World Bank, "Girls' Education." https://www.worldbank.org/en/topic/girlseducation. (last updated September 25, 2017).

World Health Organization (WHO) website, https://www.who.int/. (accessed December 28, 2018).

About the Author

Christy Mihaly writes for readers of all ages and genders. After college—where she was one of the first women to attend her formerly all-male university—she studied the law. For more than two decades, she worked as a lawyer in California and Vermont. Now she writes books under the close supervision of her dog and cat. Find out more or say hello at her website: www.christymihaly.com.

www.rourkeeducationalmedia.com

PHOTO CREDITS: Cover photo © SeventyFour | Shutterstock, drawings of faces © topform | Shutterstock.com Pages 4-5 crowd at march Editorial credit Shutterstock | bakdc, crowd with capitol in background Editorial credit Shutterstock | Erin Alexis Randolph, Page 5 Inauguration © Wangkun Jia editorial use only; page 7 © Jemastock editorial use only; page 18-19 map © capitanoproductions, African girl © Adriana Mahdalova editorial use only, Saudi woman © Mila Supinskaya Glashchenko, page 19 Malala Yousafzai © JStone editorial use only, page 20 © Dave Primov editorial use only; page 20 STOP FGM © afazuddin; page 22 © zimmytws, page 23 Iceland flag © T. Lesia, Rwanda flag © Puwadol Jaturawutthichai, Yemen flag © ASUWAN MASAE, Pakistan flag © nortongo; page 24-25 © Rena Schild; page 28-29 image showing Supreme Court and image of pro-choice protesters © Rena Schild editorial use only, pro-life protesters © Jeff McCoy editorial use only; Page 30 image with gavel © zimmytws, Page 30-31 pills © Room's Studio, ACA website © txking editorial use only; Page 32 building © Ken Wolter editorial use only; ProChoice © Linda Parton editorial use only; ProCare © a katz editorial use only; Page 33 © Rena Schild editorial use only; Page 34-35 © Sundry Photography editorial use only; office workers © Tero Vesalainen, page 36 protest sign © Karl_Sonnenberg editorial use only; page 41 poster © Everett Historical editorial use only; page 43 nurse © Monkey Business Images, Father and child © Daxiao Productions All images from Shutterstock.com except: Donald Trump portrait page 5 courtesy of the U.S. federal government; page 6 © Gage Skidmore https://creativecommons.org/licenses/©-sa/3.0/ ; page 8 Pine Leaf, Indian Heroine and Cheyenne or Arapaho woman Pretty Nose, both images Public Domain; page 10-11 color image courtesy of The Library of Congress, b/w image Public Domain image: Wikimedia; page 12 both images public domain, page 13 women suffragists courtesy of U.S. Government, Alice Paul courtesy of The Library of Congress, 19th Amendment courtesy of The National Archives; page 14 Elizabeth Balckwell courtesy of Upstate Medical University, New York, Library, Jeanette Rankin courtesy of The Library of Congress, Sally Ride courtesy of NASA, Page 15 Rosa Parks Public Domain, Fannie Lou Hamer, Betty Friedan, and Gloria Steinem photos courtesy of Library of Congress, ; page 16 © Bhbuehler https://creativecommons.org/licenses/©-sa/4.0/deed.en , page 17 Phyllis Schlafly courtesy of The Library of Congress, page 26 public domain image, source: Harvard, other images pages 26-27 courtesy of NASA; page 30 Obama and images pages 36-37 courtesy of U.S. federal government, pages 38-39 all women politician photos courtesy of U.S. Government, page 39 Billie Jean King, Public Domain author unknown; page 40 Lt. Col. Merryl Tengesdal courtesy of U.S. Air Force Photo by: Senior Airman Bob © Cummings, Airman 1st Class Natasha Lib photo courtesy of U.S. Air Force photo/Senior Airman Daniel Hughes; page 42 Hillary Clinton courtesy of National Archives and Records Administration

Edited by: Kim Thompson
Produced by Blue Door Education for Rourke Educational Media. Cover and interior design by: Jennifer Dydyk

Library of Congress PCN Data

Defining and Discussing Women's Rights / Christy Mihaly
(Shaping the Debate)
ISBN 978-1-73161-473-5 (hard cover)
ISBN 978-1-73161-280-9 (soft cover)
ISBN 978-1-73161-578-7 (e-Book)
ISBN 978-1-73161-683-8 (e-Pub)
Library of Congress Control Number: 2019932327

Rourke Educational Media
Printed in the United States of America,
North Mankato, Minnesota